W9-DED-278

NANTUCKET BASKETS

PHOTOGRAPHS BY SANDY ROCA

Nantucket Lightship Baskets

By Katherine and Edgar Seeler

Published by
The Deermouse Press
Nantucket, Massachusetts   1972

© K. & E. SEELER 1972

PUBLISHED IN U.S.A. BY THE DEERMOUSE PRESS
NANTUCKET, MASS. 02554
MANUFACTURED IN THE UNITED STATES OF AMERICA
LIBRARY OF CONGRESS CATALOGUE CARD NUMBER 76–53378
ISBN 0–9600596–3–6

NO PORTION MAY BE REPRODUCED WITHOUT
PERMISSION OF COPYRIGHT OWNERS.

SECOND EDITION, 1976
THIRD EDITION, 1981
REPRINTED, 1984

INTRODUCTION

This is a book about Nantucket Lightship Baskets. Over the years we have learned to appreciate the unusual qualities which set them apart from other baskets. At the same time there were differences in them which seemed to point to a certain progression of development which placed our baskets in a more or less chronological sequence, so that it was possible to see that they were descended from early Indian splint baskets.

We are indebted to all who have helped us, especially the following: Martha P. L. Seeler, Edouard Stackpole, José Reyes, Helen Roca-Garcia, Sandy Roca, Evelyn Kendall, Barbara Andrews, Carol Ishimoto, and Walter A. Flewelling, Jr.

The Authors

NEST OF SEVEN LIGHTSHIP BASKETS MADE IN NANTUCKET
BY CAPTAIN JAMES WYER AND DATED 1873

THE STORY OF NANTUCKET LIGHTSHIP BASKETS

Nantucket Island: whaling port, Quaker stronghold, a sandy place isolated by a location thirty miles at sea, cut off from the mainland by frequent storms and wars, this is the setting in which a unique basket tradition developed.

Almost everyone was descended from the first settlers who came in the latter part of the seventeenth century, and they were consequently so related by either blood or marriage that it was often difficult to trace the details of kinship. Coffins, Folgers, Bunkers, Gardners, Starbucks, and many other names were duplicated over and over to the despair of modern genealogists.

This closely knit character of the island community has a bearing on the creation of the Lightship Baskets of the past which are peculiar to the island, and which were the origin of the popular handbags of today. We hope to trace the early history of the Nantucket basket up to the present; for these were not "spontaneously generated" as many suppose, but they are the result of a long history of basket making on the island.

Everyone knows about the popularity of the present handbag with woven covers, made of closely woven rattan, and with a swinging handle. Travelers can recognize a fellow Nantucketer, like the woman who was leaving a crowded Paris subway and noticed a basket similar to hers being carried into the subway car. Lifting her basket high above the crowd she called out, "Nantucket?" and received a large smile and an answer as the door closed, "Oui, Nantucket."

So omnipresent are these baskets on the arms of ladies shopping on Main Street in Nantucket that one man, when asked if he knew the place, replied, "Oh, you mean that island where all the ladies carry little baskets?"

This sturdy basket is really a badge of Nantucket. The lid is usually decorated with an ivory whale or perhaps a seagull mounted on an ebony plaque, and while some cynics and humourists speak of status symbols and make class distinctions based on the use of ebony, ivory or plain wood, these baskets are without doubt the most popular product of Nantucket and a source of pride to the craftsmen who produce them, and to the people who own them.

In the early days before paper bags, cardboard, and plastic containers, baskets were a very important part of household equipment, they were used for marketing; they stored apples, potatoes, onions, and fruit; they were taken on blueberry and blackberry expeditions; they brought vegetables in from the garden; everything from eggs to wood was carried in them. Knitting and sewing baskets were universal, and baskets at their finest, appeared as ornaments. In the early household large flat baskets stored clothing and blankets.

The evolution of Nantucket baskets can very loosely be divided into six parts: first, the Indian tradition, second, the heavy duty farm baskets, third, rattan baskets, fourth, the real lightship period, fifth, the post lightship period, and sixth, the handbags of today.

The first baskets used on Nantucket were made by Indians. They were a part of the Algonquin Nation whose members, especially in New England, excelled in making splint baskets. Splints, that is long thin ribbons of wood, were made by the Indians who knew how to beat black ash logs until the wood separated into layers the thickness of a year's growth. These layers were then cut into strips, soaked in water until pliable and then woven around ribs of the same material. The bottoms of these early Indian baskets were a simple checkerboard style of weaving.

While these early Indian baskets are very different in appearance from our Nantucket Lightship Baskets, they do have many similar features. The general idea of weaving with splints is the same, although in later baskets, of course, the splint was rattan. The flange carved on the handle to keep it from slipping out is also the same though much more elaborate in later baskets. Early Indian baskets were square on the bottom, but as time went on they made an effort to change to round bottoms with the use of "spider-web" weaving.

In our collection is a dark simple Indian splint basket similar to two in the Peter Foulger Museum in Nantucket. These last are marked as made by Abram Quary who was the last man with Indian blood on the island. He died in 1854. All three baskets are simply made and have the ribs turned over at the rim and there are lacings which bind together the two rim pieces which are made of twigs only slightly carved. Here is the simple beginning of methods seen in later baskets.

We have two more baskets made by Abram Quary. One of them closely resembles the one on the table in the sad painting of Abram Quary which hangs in the Nantucket Atheneum. This little berry basket has bands of color and is beautifully made with a neat rigid handle of a carved twig which is notched under the rim. The other basket is probably a child's toy made of very fine ash splint with a rounded shape and a spider-web bottom. These old baskets speak eloquently to us of the early days and people of Nantucket.

In 1802 Indians from Mashpee on Cape Cod were coming to Nantucket to sell baskets. In "Some Early Indian Basket Makers of Southern New England" by Eva L. Butler we find this quotation about Mashpee Indians. "Although no particular individuals were named in 1802 there were many women who would 'make brooms and baskets, and sell them among their white neighbors, but more frequently carry them over to Nantucket.'"

It would appear that in those days the Nantucket Indians did not make enough baskets to keep up with the demand. At any rate Nantucket people were familiar with the early Indian splint baskets.

Indian baskets were for the most part, fragile; used for berrypicking and storing herbs or for putting away blankets and clothing, they did not have the strength needed by farmers for heavier duties such as carrying apples or potatoes. So the farmers began to look about for stronger baskets. Sometimes the Indians made them, and other times the farmers themselves, taught by the Indians, began to make them in the winter months. Others made it a year-round business taking their products from farm to farm in wagons.

In Sandwich, New Hampshire, there were many basketmakers and the Fogg family were famous for this, each time a member married into another family it would turn to basketmaking. One man who was a shoemaker went from house to house not only tending to shoes but also selling baskets.

Most of these durable farm baskets had cleverly made bottoms woven into a spider-web that was created as the ribs crossed over. Some baskets had wooden plank bottoms like those in Nantucket Lightship baskets with a sawed groove into which the ribs could fit. A large and well-developed bail handle was attached in several clever ways, frequently to an ear which was inserted into the basket about half or three-quarters down the side. This was the method used in Nantucket Lightship Baskets.

The materials for these farm baskets were ash, hickory and oak and were "rived" or cut from logs and peeled smooth with the use of a shaving horse and drawknives, an improvement on the laborious method of obtaining splint by beating logs in Indian fashion.

During at least the first half of the nineteenth century splint bottomed chairs were very popular which meant that the material for baskets was produced in abundance. One Hiram Corliss of Sandwich, New Hampshire split and wove brown ash into baskets and also made hundreds of chair seats.

There are some of these baskets on Nantucket, and there is no doubt they were made there. They are a link between the Indian baskets and the rattan baskets which in turn became the lightship baskets. We have a basket similar to several seen on Nantucket that so closely resembles a lightship basket it is hard to believe that it is not one. Yet there is no use of rattan and the bottom is a woven spider-web, not a wooden plank. Yet the neatly shaped ears, the handle attached by a copper rivet and washer, and the fine quality and charm of shape all make us realize its close connection with our modern baskets.

Two other baskets linking the farm baskets to the lightship baskets have wooden bottoms and although most of their weavers are of hickory splint, the bottom few rows are of heavy rattan. And some of the pieces of the rim are also rattan.

This use of the wooden bottom and of rattan leads us to the third section in the evolution of the history of lightship baskets. Sometime probably in the 1830's and 1840's this type of sturdy basket with hickory splints and woven bottom changed, with the use of rattan and wooden bottoms, into the style which would eventually be known far and wide as a style peculiar to Nantucket.

It is useful now to describe the characteristics that make the Nantucket Lightship Basket so unique. First in importance is the fact that the baskets are woven of rattan. This strong material comes from a climbing vine of the palm family. It is the genus Calamus and has a solid stem and grows in tropical countries, such as the Philippines, China and India. Rattan, or cane as it is often called, was used for chair seats, replacing the older hickory splints, so it was available to basketmakers. Since Nantucketers had close contact with the Pacific it could also come directly to the island.

The second and very important characteristic of a Nantucket Lightship Basket is the use of wooden bottoms. As we have seen the farm baskets of New Hampshire and other New England states sometimes had wooden bottoms, but there is no doubt that the Nantucket basket-makers were the first to use this strong type of bottom exclusively in their product. Ribs of the basket are inserted deeply into an incised groove and the result is not only a very strong basket but one that eliminates the difficulties of weaving an intricate spider-web. The ribs could be much shorter in this method. Hand carved pieces of pine appear in the earlier baskets, but harder wood turned on the lathe soon replaced this. Almost any type of wood was used, for living on an island makes people clever at adapting what is at hand. So the bottom of a basket in the birthplace of Maria Mitchell has printed on it "Merchants Tobacco Company No. 8 Fifth Co Dist Boston Mass." Boxes, planks, even old kitchen chopping boards went into the baskets.

The third element peculiar to these baskets is the use of molds on which to weave them. Indians, Shakers and others did use molds, but again it was so universal on Nantucket that it gives a very distinct appearance. Not only does the basket remain more steady but using a mold produces accuracy in size so nests of baskets could be made. The molds were made from anything, pieces of ship masts for instance, and in the case of large sizes they were made up of several pieces.

Now these three elements of Nantucket Lightship Baskets, the use of rattan, the wooden bottoms, and employing molds are concrete subjects easy to discuss, but the fourth quality is that elusive appearance which is compounded of many things, and this is more difficult to present. The narrow well carved handles attached to ears of distinctive design, the skillful tight weaving with ribs close together and tapered, and the firm, but graceful sturdiness, all this combines to present an artistic result and a unique identity. This is the result of the fact that these baskets were made by a group in an isolated community of families closely connected. As we have said the families of Nantucket were inter-related to the point of confusion, so methods and knowledge would be shared resulting in a very homogeneous product.

Shaker communities made baskets with similar uniform qualities as their group was also isolated and closely-knit, but this was due to religious reasons. We must not make the mistake of an earlier writer who confused Shakers with the Quakers of Nantucket. There is no evidence that Nantucket baskets were connected with the Shaker baskets. The Shakers learned basketry directly from the Indians and they show this, being fragile and using the same materials as the Indians. On the other hand the Nantucket baskets progressed a long way from the simple Indian baskets.

We can understand the four characteristics that set Nantucket Lightship Baskets apart—the use of rattan, the wooden bottoms, the use of molds, and the special homogeneous quality of beauty and workmanship, but we also want to know who made them and how. We are fortunate in having two voices from the past to tell us something about this. More than a hundred years ago a little boy sat with men in his father's shop on Nantucket watching baskets being made, and what he has to say is more interesting than anything we could ferret out for ourselves today. This little boy was Joseph E. C. Farnham who wrote his delightful book "Brief Data and Memories of My Boyhood Days in Nantucket." The quotation which follows refers to his experiences about the year 1854.

"Another quite material business, on the side, at the shop of my father, —indulged in for pleasure rather than for profit,—was basket making. That was done mostly in the colder seasons of the year. That little iron cylinder stove, radiating its comforting heat, was a magnet around which a number of men used to sit and indulge in that occupation. Of them I well recall the genial Capt. George F. Joy, and the ever pleasant and agreeable Mr. Charles G. Coggeshall. Each of them worked while 'pulling' upon one of the then so popular 'T. D.' clay pipes, evidently fully enjoying the smoke derived therefrom. I delighted to sit and listen to their entertaining conversation and story-telling. A boy then ten to twelve years of age, I soon learned, under their tutelage, the art of making those baskets,—for art it really was,—and I now possess one which I made so many years ago. The basket work done by those men was truly of a superior class, and their product was pleasingly attractive. We called them rattan baskets. They were made in varying sizes, from very small up to about the capacity of a peck. In slight graduation from about a quart in size up through five or six sizes those baskets were placed one within the other in so-called 'nests.' As so arranged they made a most inviting appearance. 'Work-baskets' for the ladies were made quite large over and were woven about six or eight inches high, with a woven cover, hinged at the side, and they were certainly very neat and pretty. I did not then, because so young and the sight so familiar to me, think of that pleasurable exercise, with its utilitarian results, as I do now in retrospect. Those men, some of them retired from service at sea on a whale-ship, others temporarily idle, most profitably employed their spare hours in the manner narrated. Practical, as those products indeed were, they merit, also, to rank with the truly artistic.

"Those baskets were made principally of rattan or 'cane,' such as is used for chair seats. First, a wooden bottom of adaptable size to the basket to be made, was turned in a lathe, with a slot or groove cut in all around at its outer edge in which to insert the 'ribs;' those ribs were fashioned from large split cane, carrying the round edge on the outer side, with the flat surface on the inner; concaved and thinned at the lower end, they were placed quite closely together in the groove of the wooden bottom; then, with the ribs standing straight out all around, the whole was placed over an empty pail or similar vessel of proper size. With a sponge of boiling water those 'ribs' were quite thoroughly soaked, and were then gradually forced down into the pail, causing them to incline upward, a string was tied around them in that form, and then all was set away to dry for a few hours, usually over night; when taken from the pail and released from the string the ribs would be somewhat inclined in the direction required, and upon them the weaving of the basket was begun, using the fine rattan cane, by inserting one end in beside one of those ribs, and then carrying it over and under them, back and forth, drawing it taut, all the while shaping and forming the basket, a firm finish and symmetry was attained; the next process was the binding off at the top, which was done with thin outer and inner hoops, each round on one side and flat on the other, made from white-oak, and secured in place by the same material of which the basket was constructed criss-crossed around and about them; at opposite sides of the basket was an 'ear' run down between the hoops, following one of the ribs on each side and within the weaving, each ear being fastened to the hoops with a brass rivet; a nicely smoothed half-rounded swinging bail was attached to each of the two ears by a brass rivet,—the ears and bail were also wrought from white-oak; a thin coat of light varnish gave the finishing touch. Surely those baskets, made, as described, so many years ago, were of rare workmanship. They were useful and were highly prized.

"To some extent, possibly, such baskets were and are made in other localities. I am quite sure, however, that such are not now made as a side issue by men in shops, similar to the shop of my father, as I have narrated. On board the Nantucket South Shoal Lightship, and amid other similar close environment, baskets of the character named are now quite plentifully and artistically made for profit by the crew of such an isolated vessel,—hence the name 'lightship baskets' now given them. It is now a number of years since a Nantucket man has been one of the crew of 'South Shoals' so all of the baskets offered for sale in the Nantucket shops during the summer months are made by a half dozen men who devote their spare time to making the baskets, the art having been handed down from generation to generation. The baskets are still made in 'nests,' and are on sale in the shops of Nantucket. Summer tourists to the island town appreciate and buy them as souvenirs of their visit."

This delightful account of making baskets in the early 1850's describes the process much as it is today except for the substitution of wooden molds for buckets and a few other refinements.

It is of interest to us that work baskets with woven covers were made, a premonition of the handbags to come one hundred years later. Also this is the period of rattan ribs and we have eight baskets of this type in our collection. They are very strong looking with very pleasing texture and color caused by the use of rattan ribs as well as weavers. However, most makers apparently preferred hickory or oak ribs, and most baskets continued to be made with these.

Farnham does not refer to making the handles, but this was a laborious job which involved splitting out strips from green logs, reducing them to proper size with a drawknife, and shaping and smoothing with a spokeshave. They were then bent to shape and tied and hung up to dry. If the wood was dry it was steamed or boiled to soften it.

Farnham's description gives us a realistic picture of these men, many of them whalers accustomed to long months of male companionship at sea, sitting around a stove working and talking. No doubt wives were glad their husbands could keep busy although one story told to us years ago by an old Nantucketer gives another side. She said when her grandfather came back to the house with his first basket he said to his wife, "How do you like my basket?" and she replied, "Well, I guess it'll go fer one." We were told that ever after in that family they were know as "gofer baskets."

In his book "Scrimshaw and Scrimshanders Whales and Whalemen" E. Norman Flayderman says that Nantucket baskets were the only example of this craft developed and practiced by the white man. He claims all other basket weaving has come from primitive non-white races. The basketmakers of England and Europe should not be eliminated so casually. While as a matter of fact the Indians really did influence the trend of Nantucket baskets.

It is surely possible that the whalers saw some of the fine basket weaving in China and the Philippines; and this might have encouraged them to try rattan, but it is possible, also, that some rattan baskets were made on the mainland, perhaps in New Hampshire. We have two made entirely of rattan with spider-web bottoms and rigid handles; they might have been made about the same time as those discussed by Farnham, but they are the only two we have ever seen.

But to go back to the fascinating description painted by Farnham of these men of the sea meeting for sociability as well as basket making. They were called rattan baskets, he says, and not lightship baskets which was a name that was applied later to those actually made on board. However, so romantic is the name "Lightship Basket", conjuring up the lonely life of men on a ship anchored on the dangerous shoals off Nantucket, with nothing to do but tend the light and make baskets day after day, that no one would dare suggest the name be changed even for those baskets made on land. Lightship Baskets they should remain whether made on land or sea.

There is another description of basketmaking in the book, "My House and I" by Mary Eliza Starbuck. She tells about the workshop in their house where her stepfather made Nantucket Lightship Baskets. She says that he made workbaskets and egg baskets and whole nests of seven. This is particularly interesting to us as we have a nest of seven baskets owned by her and signed by J. Wyer who was the stepfather she is talking about. The date 1873 is carved on the bottom with his name. He was master of the ship Spartan. When we walk by the old Walter Folger house on Pleasant Street, we think of stepfather working away there with such dexterity in his "shop-chamber" just a hundred years ago.

At the same time that these baskets were being made as described by Farnham and Miss Starbuck, they were also being produced at sea on the lightship, properly called No. 1, Nantucket, New South Shoal, which was established twenty-four miles south of Sankaty Light in 1856. This is a predecessor of the ship we see as we approach New York from abroad, only she has been moved to a new place since the days we are writing about. Here ten people, in a space about one hundred and three feet by twenty-five feet, lived and took care of the two lights which burned so brightly with sixteen lamps. With nothing to do but clean the lamps and stand watch, they made baskets probably continuing what some of them had been doing on land. No doubt partly because of their isolation, they made some of the finest baskets ever seen. Durable, closely woven, graceful, and beautifully balanced those made on the South Shoal cannot be surpassed.

Some interesting facts are written by G. Kobbe about his visit to the South Shoal Lightship in Century Magazine for August, 1891. He describes the rough trip out to the ship and then he says that on board the routine is very simple and aside to lowering, cleaning and hoisting the lights and standing watch there are no other duties. Each member of the crew is aboard for eight months. The captain receives one thousand dollars, the mate seven hundred dollars, and each of the crew six hundred dollars.

This article goes on to say, "A number of stores in Nantucket sell what are known as lightship-baskets. They come in 'nests,' consisting of five or eight baskets of various sizes fitting one into the other. These baskets are made only on the South Shoal Lightship. Their manufacture has been attempted ashore, but has never paid. This is because there is a very narrow margin of profit in them for the lightship crew, who make them chiefly for the purpose of whiling away the weary winter hours. In summer the crew occupies its spare time 'scrimshawing,' an old whaling term for doing ingenious mechanical work, having aboard the South Shoal the special meaning of preparing the strips of wood and ratan for the manufacture of baskets in winter. The bottoms are turned ashore. The blocks over which the baskets are made have been aboard the ship since she was first anchored off the New South Shoal in 1856. The sides of the baskets are of white oak or hickory, filled in with ratan, and they are round or oval, of graceful lines and great durability, the sizes to a nest ranging from a pint to a peck and a half."

It is extremely interesting that scrimshawing on board the South Shoal meant preparing the material for making baskets. The use of this word by Mr. Kobbe was misinterpreted by several writers to mean that the carving of ivory scrimshaw was regularly done on the lightship.

There was said to be a lathe on board the lightship, but perhaps by the time Mr. Kobbe visited the ship bottoms were made on land as he says.

His observation about the baskets being five or eight is different from what Miss Starbuck says about the nest being seven baskets. Actually although seven seems to be the number used by later makers, probably any number might be used, depending on the individual maker. After all, the convenience of placing a basket inside another one was very great when cupboard and closet space was very scarce. In many Nantucket houses, except for a few shelves, a buttery, and perhaps one closet off the front hall, there was no extra space at all.

Although in the beginning the South Shoal Lightship was manned entirely by Nantucket men, by 1905, the last one, Charlie Sylvia had left. This undoubtedly accounts for the fact that baskets were no longer made on the lightship, rather than that a directive from the government ordered them to stop.

So with the close of the nineteenth century the fourth period of Nantucket basketry, the lightship period, comes to an end. But baskets were still made on land, especially by those who had left the lightship like W. D. Appleton who continued in his shop on lower Orange Street until some time around 1910.

It is a sad fact that very few of the baskets are marked by the makers but there are some labels pasted on, such as the one that says "Made on Board, South Shoals Lightship, by W. D. Appleton."

Some of the names associated with baskets made on the South Shoal are: Captain Charles B. Ray (who completed his 200th rattan basket in November, 1866), Captain Andrew Sandsbury, Captain David E. Ray, Captain Thomas James, Davis Hall, Uriah Manter, Joe Fisher, Charlie Sylvia, S. B. Raymond, George Swain, W. D. Appleton.

The days of people who knew whaling ships and the old traditions of producing things by hand were over, but the art of making baskets in the old style did not die out in Nantucket. For one thing, the tourist trade was increasing and there was a good market for something local and with some tradition of the sea behind it. W. D. Appleton had taught A. D. Williams who was selling baskets at 120 Orange Street.

We have a small beautifully made basket with a woven lid fastened by a brass hinge which is labelled on the bottom, "Light Ship Basket, made by A. D. Williams 120 Orange St. Nantucket, Mass. Nov. 17, 1918." A larger basket is the same only the date is 1923. These baskets with woven covers foreshadow, if only dimly, the modern handbag. Williams also made very fine nests of seven baskets, both round and oval, and fine waste baskets. His label is mistakenly read as Atkins in Flayderman's book.

Ferdinand Sylvaro was making baskets at this time, and he lived at 97 Orange Street. W. M. Gibbs also made baskets marked with paper labels saying, "Manufactured by W. M. Gibbs, Nantucket, Mass." He is erroneously reported in Flayderman's book as "Bibbs—Nantucket."

One of the most prolific basketmakers of this post lightship period was Mitchell Ray who made strong sturdy wastebaskets, nests both oval and round, and a variety of other shapes and sizes. It was his grandfather Charles B. Ray who had made 200 baskets by November, 1866. So "Mitchy" as everyone called him, came into this craft by inheritance. His label reads: "Made by Mitchell Ray Nantucket, Mass." Sometimes he included the well-known rhyme: "I was made on Nantucket, I'm strong and I'm stout, Don't lose me or burn me and I'll never wear out."

Sherwin Boyer was another maker of this period and his label was merely a stencil with his name spelled twice, vertically and horizontally, crossing at the letter Y. He made shoulder bags with leather tops in about 1950.

Now we have reached the culmination of about one hundred and fifty years of making baskets on Nantucket Island. Beginning with the simple Indian baskets, and going from them to the heavier and more useful farm baskets, we progressed to the "rattan baskets" made on land and from them to the Lightship Baskets actually made on board the South Shoal Lightship. It should be mentioned that although we have one basket said to be made on the Cross Rip, we have no evidence at present to prove that any were made in the old days except on the

South Shoal. In the 1950's some were made on the Cross Rip. The fifth group of baskets we discussed were those made after 1910, especially in the 1920's and 1930's for tourists who appreciated their fine workmanship and usefulness. It is of course difficult to draw a fine line between these periods; they shade into each other and overlap sometimes in puzzling ways. But at the same time, each group does seem to have distinct characteristics and these will become more apparent in a study of the photographic plates to follow.

José Formoso Reyes came to Nantucket Island from the Philippine Islands in 1945. Disappointed in not obtaining a teaching position, he turned to basket making as a livelihood. A highly educated man, he also had great skill as a craftsman and the ability needed to popularize the handbags he created until they became the most sought after product of Nantucket Island.

In 1948 among many baskets of different shapes and sizes he made a small basket with a woven lid to be used for a handbag. He showed this to Charlie Sayle whose wife suggested that her husband put one of his small black whales on the wooden piece in the middle of the top. Mr. Sayle for some time had been carving whale pins. This was the beginning of the handbag we know today.

Since then many different carvers from Nantucket have supplied the decoration for the tops of the baskets, and Mr. Reyes has added ivory latches, and pins and dowels of ivory to the handles of the baskets.

In recent years many amateurs have made lightship baskets on Nantucket, two of the best being Bunt Mackay and Irving Burnside. At present there are supposed to be at least nine people making baskets, some of them full-time professionals.

The men of old Nantucket who sat weaving in friendly groups around a potbellied stove, or on the lonely lightship, would surely be surprised to know how valuable their baskets have become nor could they believe how much they are appreciated and treasured.

DESCRIPTION OF PLATE I

An Indian basket from Nantucket, typical of the small berry picking baskets made by the Algonquin Indians of New England. It is made entirely of ash splints which the Indians pounded from logs of black ash. This broke the large spring cells so that the more dense summer wood came off in thin layers. It shows the typical Indian method of weaving with one wide band and one narrow band. The bottom is also typical with checkerboard weaving.

The rim is merely two half round twigs bound together, and the handle, inserted into the basket three-quarters of the way down the sides, is also a shaped twig, carved so that there is a lip or flange under the rim to prevent slipping.

The two baskets like this in the Peter Foulger Museum in Nantucket are both marked Abram Quary. We do not know who made this basket but it is a touching reminder of Indian life on the Island.

Diameter 5 inches   Height 4 inches

DESCRIPTION OF PLATE 2

The larger basket was woven by Abram Quary, the last man with Indian blood to live on Nantucket, who died in 1854. There is a similar basket in the painting of him which hangs in the Nantucket Atheneum. It is a typical Indian shape, round top and square woven bottom. There are four bands of brown colored splints for decoration. The ribs are bent back over the top weaver alternately inside and outside as is usual with Indian baskets as well as other early splint baskets. This gives a firmer edge to the basket and keeps the upper row of weaving from slipping off. This method of turning over the end of the ribs can be seen in some of the early Nantucket baskets.

Diameter 6 inches   Height 4½ inches

The smaller basket was also made by Abram Quary, of fine ash splint and is distinguished by its round spider-web woven bottom. The ribs are cleverly tapered at both ends to give a rounded, bulging effect to the sides. It was probably made to be sold as a child's toy.

Diameter 4 inches   Height 3¼ inches

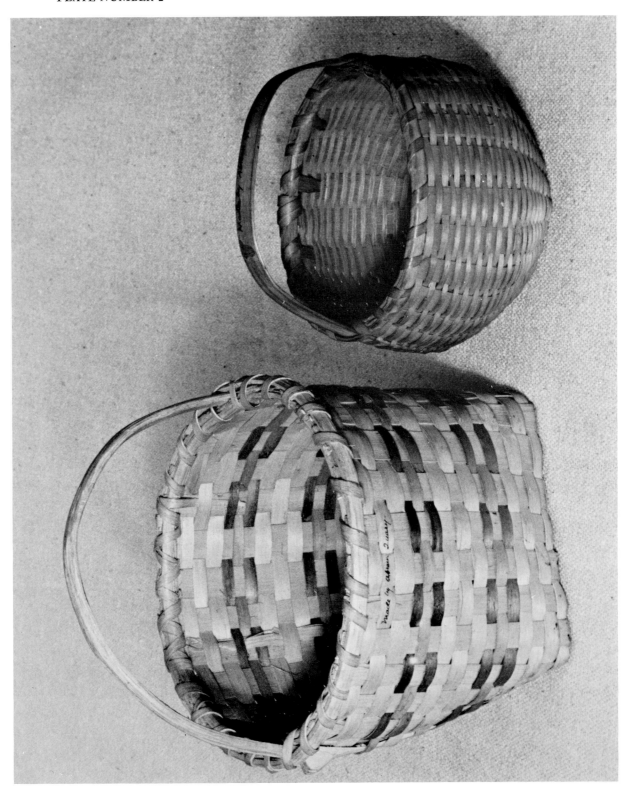

DESCRIPTION OF PLATE 3

An Indian basket of smooth ash splint with square checkerboard bottom. The rim is made of an ash splint on the outside and a smoothed twig on the inside. The handle is inserted inside the basket to the bottom and the flange under the rim is on the inside. Indian women usually wove these finer baskets, the men making the stronger and coarser ones.

This could have been made on Nantucket, where it was purchased some fifty years ago, or it might have been brought over by Indians from the mainland. There is mention of the Mashpees coming over from Cape Cod as early as 1802. The well shaped notch under the rim and the larger ribs and finer weavers foretell the more sturdy and elaborate lightship baskets.

The name Lottie Handford is written in pencil on the bottom, presumably the name of the owner.

Diameter 6 ¾ inches   Height 5 ½ inches

DESCRIPTION OF PLATE 4

An old Indian basket used by Indians and others for storing clothing and blankets. Beautifully made with checkerboard bottom and even, close weaving on the sides, it is similar to one in the Peter Foulger Museum except for the loop handles which in our basket are more skillfully made. They are similar to other handles on Indian baskets, being inserted half way down the basket, and leaving three inches of the neatly carved wood showing outside the weaving. In the carved top which allows thinner wood for the bent portion, these handles resemble those on waste baskets made perhaps a hundred years later by Mitchell Ray and other Nantucketers. This type of basket appears in the oil painting of Abram Quary in the Atheneum and is used for herbs and dried plants.

Length 18 inches   Width 15 ¾ inches   Height 8 inches

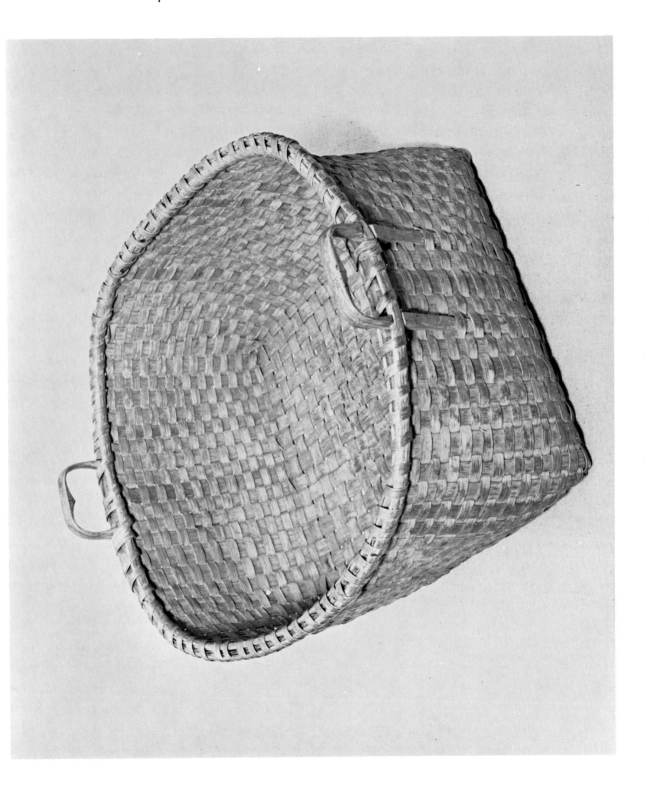

24

DESCRIPTION OF PLATE 5

A heavier type of Indian basket made for the use of white farmers and possibly made by the farmers after lessons from the Indians. To accommodate the desire of the white people for round baskets the Indians began to weave spider-web and double spider-web bottoms. The ribs are larger than before but still turned over at the top and the handles are rigid but with more carefully carved lips inserted on the inside of the basket. The lacing of the rim becomes more careful and the weavers are of uniform size, so that slowly the appearance of the basket is changing to one more familiar to us.

Although this basket was purchased over half a century ago on Nantucket, we have no real way of knowing where it was made or by whom. But it shows much of the Indian methods with a beginning of some elusive change. Indians marrying into white families often brought their basket-making skill into the family who also learned the craft. Gradually these baskets emerged as a special group of farm baskets, many of them large and heavy, and made by special basketmakers in New Hampshire, Massachusetts and elsewhere.

Diameter 8 inches   Height 6 inches

DESCRIPTION OF PLATE 6

A typical farm basket from New Hampshire of smooth ash splint. The wooden bottom is the same as that used in the Nantucket baskets and the ribs are inserted into a sawed groove in the edge of the bottom in the same way.

The swinging handle or bail is attached in a very ingenious manner by heavy wooden loops. A less cumbersome method appears in the following plate which is more like the Nantucket baskets.

Nantucket had close connections with New Hampshire and must have known these baskets which do resemble in a crude way, the better and more finished lightship baskets. The wooden bottom made tighter weaving possible as well as allowing the use of shorter ribs.

Diameter 12 inches   Height 8 ½ inches

DESCRIPTION OF PLATE 7

A heavy-duty farm basket showing the moveable handle or bail similar to Nantucket baskets. This one was made in New Hampshire or Massachusetts and retains the checkerboard weaving on the bottom and the ribs bent over at the rim which is reminiscent of Indian work. The ribs and weavers are heavy ash splint beaten off a black ash log in Indian fashion. Some of the weavers are of 2 layers, each one a year's growth. The lacing of the rim is of smoothed ash.

Except for the rivet and washer, there is not a nail in the basket. The wooden ear to which the handle is attached is very nicely carved and shaped and is on the inside of the basket. In general this method of attaching the handle resembles the lightship baskets although in the more carefully made Nantucket baskets the carving was more delicate.

Diameter 13 inches   Height 9 ½ inches

DESCRIPTION OF PLATE 8

This delicate basket of hickory splint from Nantucket resembles the lightship baskets; closely woven, the bail handle neatly shaped and connected to a well carved ear with a lip under the rim, careful criss-cross lacing of the rim, all combine to make this look like a real Nantucket lightship basket. However there is no rattan and no wooden bottom; there is a spider-web bottom and the ends of the ribs turned over (see to left of lip under rim) in the old style.

There are other baskets similar to this on the island, but we have no knowledge at all of their creators.

Diameter 8 ¼ inches   Height 5 ¼ inches

DESCRIPTION OF PLATE 9

A strong beautiful hickory splint egg basket from Nantucket. An unusual feature is the extremely wide ribs in the center of the bottom which are narrowed as they go up the sides of the basket only to get wider at the rim.

The rattan lacing of the rim replaces an older one which was probably not rattan. There is a gap between the inner and outer rim pieces which is typical of the earlier baskets. In the later and more finished ones, a cover of rattan is placed over this.

In order to make the odd number necessary for this spider-web bottom, one rib is split into three, all other ribs are split in two.

The initials E. R. F. branded into the handle are probably those of the owner.

Diameter 12 ¾ inches   Height 4 ¾ inches

34

This is a very important early Nantucket basket showing the first use of rattan. It is seen in the weavers of the three bottom rows and in the lacing of the rim. The inside rim piece is also rattan. There is a hand carved wooden pine bottom into which the hickory ribs are fitted and nailed on the inside with fine nails, one to each rib.

The ribs are still folded over on the outside. The rib on which the handle is mounted terminates above in a thick ear. There is a criss-cross lacing of the rim.

A sturdy, handsome basket which forecasts the later ones made entirely of rattan weavers.

Diameter 8 ¼ inches   Height 6 inches

DESCRIPTION OF PLATE I I

A smaller hickory splint basket similar to the preceding plate. This also shows the beginning use of rattan in the four rows at the bottom of the basket. Both pieces of the rim are made of rattan. The ribs are nailed into the hand cut wooden pine bottom with twenty-three small nails, one for each rib. In this basket the ear is a separate piece of wood distinct from the ribs and inserted into the basket, the method used later on. An over-lapped lacing is used.

Hickory splints were made and sold by Indians for both chair seats and baskets so were easy to obtain in the first half of the 19th century and even later.

Diameter 6 ½ inches   Height 5 ¼ inches

DESCRIPTION OF PLATE 12

A beautiful strong early Nantucket basket using all rattan weavers. The wide hickory splint ribs are nailed to the bottom which is of pine and is turned on a lathe. Criss-cross lacings of rattan hold the hickory rim together.

Copper rivets with handmade washers connect the handle to the simple earpieces so that it resembles the farm baskets.

The large rattan weavers give the basket a very handsome primitive appearance, and it is sturdy and durable.

The name T. C. Defriez branded into the handle and also the bottom on the outside is probably an indication of ownership rather than the maker's name. He was a ship captain born in Nantucket in 1822.

Diameter 10 inches   Height 7 ¾ inches

DESCRIPTION OF PLATE 13

A small old basket of unusual shape. The bottom of checkerboard weaving is reminiscent of Indian work. Each hickory splint is split to make the fine ribs. The weavers are all fine rattan and the rim pieces of hickory splint are laced with simple overlap of rattan.

The two handles are set in very firmly. Was this a yarn basket, a child's doll wash basket, or a storage place for small objects? We can never know, but it was surely treasured by someone on Nantucket.

Length 10¼ inches   Width 8½ inches   Height 4¼ inches

DESCRIPTION OF PLATE 14

A very attractive small basket with rattan weavers. The ribs, rim pieces, and handle are all of hickory. The nailed pine bottom is hand made and painted green outside. There is a very delicately carved ear with a pronounced lip under the rim.

It is possible to see the overlap of a rib just to the left of the ear. Later on this method of turning over the rib, which strengthened the basket, was given up and the ribs were nailed to the rim.

Although small, it is a part of the evolution of Nantucket lightship baskets as well as a charming example of basketry.

Diameter 5 inches   Height 3 ¼ inches

44

Another small basket made by the same person as Plate 14. This, however, has all rattan ribs and rim as well as weavers, and foreshadows the all rattan baskets which come later.

That this is an early basket is proved by the fact that some of the ribs are turned over at the top in the old way, and that there is no rattan strip covering the crack in the rim. This was probably made before 1850.

By this time rattan, or cane as it was often called, was popular for weaving chair seats.

Diameter 5 ½ inches   Height 3 ¾ inches

DESCRIPTION OF PLATE 16

Small and closely woven, this basket illustrates an attempt to weave the rattan very tight. The hickory splint ribs are scarcely visible. The walnut bottom is turned. A maple handle is attached in an unusual way with wooden ears covered with copper and attached to the copper ends of the handle.

This basket exactly fits the lathe turned pine mold probably made from a piece of a ship's mast.

Although the basket is rather crudely made, perhaps someone's first attempt, it has a certain naive appeal.

Diameter 6½ inches   Height 4½ inches

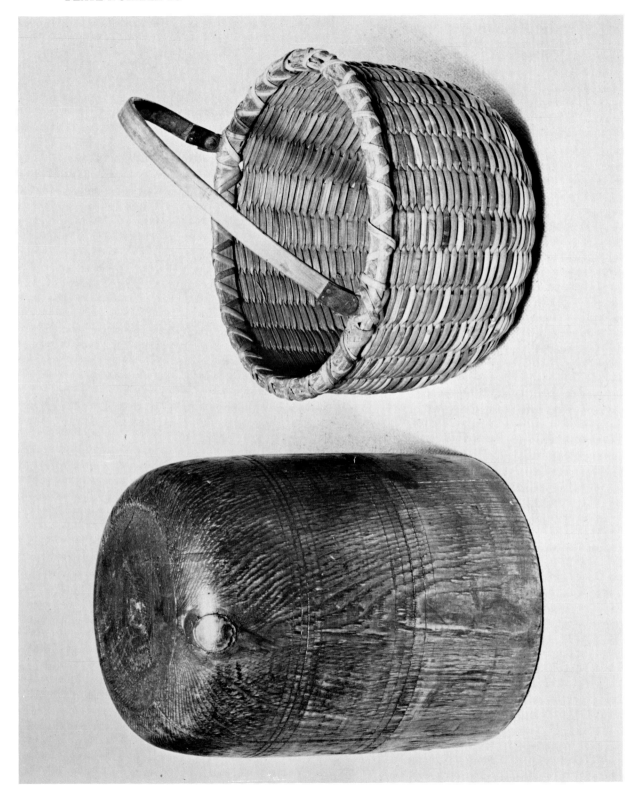

DESCRIPTION OF PLATE 17

A delicately made basket with two distinct features. The rim includes a middle strip, between the outside and inside pieces. This serves to cover the rib ends which are no longer turned over, and it also prevents dirt from getting into the crack between the two rim pieces. Also, nails are used as well as lacing to keep the rim intact.

The maple bottom is made by hand. Four shades of rattan give a decorative appearance. This is a typical early lightship basket and could have been made either on board or on land. The inch and a half of wood showing below the ear is typical of earlier baskets. The criss-cross lacing is very carefully executed.

Diameter 7 ¼ inches   Height 4 ¾ inches

DESCRIPTION OF PLATE 18

The smallest basket from an old nest of three (or possibly more). This illustrates the increasing use of rattan, in the weavers, lacing of the rim, and rim pieces. The pine bottom has been painted green and the hickory ribs are nailed into it. These ribs are not of equal width and the basket has a primitive appearance which is very pleasing.

The rounded hickory ears are carved to hold the rim.

It is interesting to contrast this basket with those made later on the South Shoal Lightship; this one so carelessly but sturdily put together, the later ones with such finished perfection. But probably only thirty years, if that, separate the two.

Diameter 9 inches   Height 6 ¼ inches

DESCRIPTION OF PLATE 19

The early nest of three baskets referred to in the preceding plate. The fact that all three bottoms are nailed, the rattan lacings are carried far down the side of the basket, there are no nails used in the rim, the ear has a piece of wood showing beneath the rim, and there is a rim cover in only the smallest basket, all indicate the early period of the nest.

The maker used rattan for only some of the rim pieces as if trying something new. The shiny rattan weavers produce a more finished appearance than hickory.

These are extremely handsome examples of early Nantucket baskets, and worthy ancestors of the lightship baskets and the modern handbag.

Diameter 10¼ inches   Height 7 inches

DESCRIPTION OF PLATE 20

A curious all rattan basket from Massachusetts, this is the only example of the use of this material from the mainland that we have seen. The rigid handle and inside rim are made of oak. The heavy rattan ribs are peeled and thinned so they can be folded over at the rim in the traditional way.

The bottom is carefully woven in an indented spider-web. While this basket is not important in the family history of lightship baskets, it is intriguing as a product using the same material. The rattan used is very large and produced an extremely strong basket skillfully designed. Nothing is known about this basket but it is possible it was made about 1850.

Diameter 11½ inches   Height 8½ inches

DESCRIPTION OF PLATE 21

This is the smallest of an early nest of three baskets which is made of rattan weavers and rattan ribs. Early baskets had ribs of ash, then hickory, both obtainable because they were popular for chair seats. Now these baskets have ribs of rattan and are the type made in the 1850's as described by Farnham in his book "Brief Historical Data and Memories of My Boyhood Days in Nantucket."

The bottom is handmade of pine and the initials "W S Ch" are carved in it. "William S. Chase" is also written below it in ink.

An interesting feature is that the ear is part of an oak rib extending into the bottom. There is a rattan strip covering the opening between the two oak rim pieces.

The handle is nicely shaped oak; "Mary P. Worth" is written on it.

The middle basket of this nest is exactly the same only the price "$15" is written on the bottom. The largest basket has a maple bottom on which is carved "A G H". In ink is written "made by A. G. Hussey", and the price "$10". The ribs are fastened to the bottom with copper tacks only in the largest basket.

These are strong and sturdy baskets and with the use of rattan ribs as well as weavers there is a delightful color and shine.

Diameters 7¾ inches   9½ inches   11¼ inches

Heights 6 inches   7 inches   8¼ inches

This large sewing basket has rattan ribs and weavers of almost the same size. The mahogany bottom appears to have been made from a chopping board.

Criss-cross lacings and small tacks on the inside hold the rim pieces together and the rim cover of rattan is wider than usual. The rim pieces are of oak and each one would have to be 46 inches long to go around and lap over.

There are two rattan covered ring handles fastened under the rim opposite each other. Durable and rugged it must have seen a great deal of use.

Diameter 12 ¾ inches   Height 5 ¼ inches

DESCRIPTION OF PLATE 23

Another basket with rattan ribs as well as weavers. The rim of maple has neat criss-cross lacings and the handle is also of maple.

Although no nails show, it is obvious from the small cracks at the top of the ribs that they were nailed to the inner rim and then covered by the outer rim.

The most interesting feature of this basket is that the nicely carved maple ears are not inserted into the rim as in all other baskets, but they are on the inside with a notch to fit the rim. Because of this the bail handle is attached on the outside of the ears.

The bottom is mahogany and "M. E. Gardner" in old-fashioned letters appears there. The fact that there is no hole in the middle of the bottom indicates that it was not fastened to a mold during its construction.

Diameter 9¼ inches   Height 6¼ inches

DESCRIPTION OF PLATE 24

Another basket with rattan ribs and weavers made by a careful workman. There are two oak ribs ending in well shaped ears. Placing a rib in this way took planning and skill.

The handle is oak. The black walnut bottom has Harrison Gardner branded inside and the price "$15" is on the outside. The name probably refers to the owner in this case as Harrison Gardner was a farmer on Nantucket. Like some New Hampshire farmers he might well have made baskets in the winter but usually names on these early baskets refer to the owner. The maker, proud of his work as he must have been, seldom left his name; but the owner, fearful of losing his basket at a church supper or meeting, frequently marked his basket.

These "rattan baskets" as Farnham says they were called are all extremely well made and beautiful.

Diameter 11½ inches   Height 7 inches

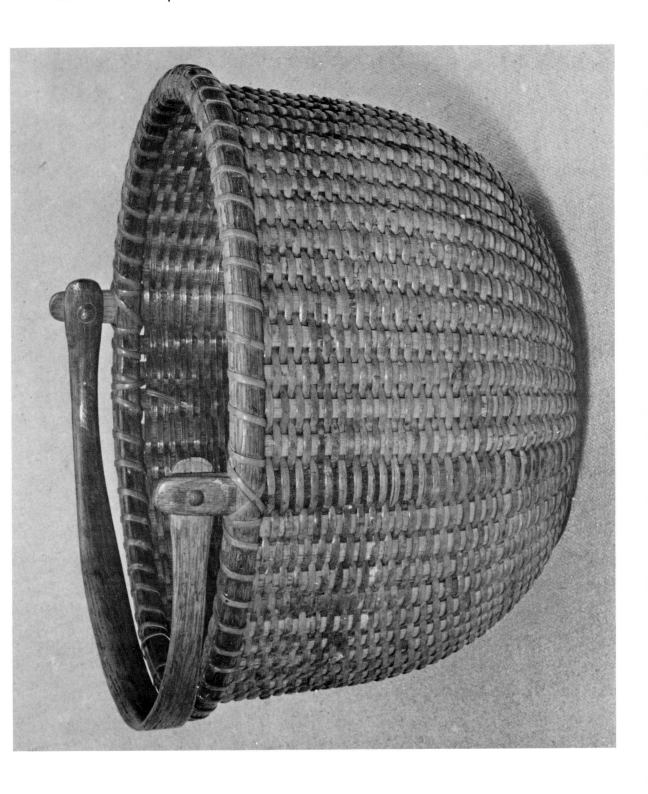

DESCRIPTION OF PLATE 25

This small basket has fine rattan ribs as well as weavers and the ears appear at the end of oak ribs as in the previous plate. The ribs are fastened to the inside rim by tacks and then they are covered by the outer rim, leaving the impression that no nails are used.

This probably was made on a mold, and the mahogany bottom is decorated with turned rings inside. We cannot prove these are identification marks except in a few cases.

It was not until José Reyes started making his baskets in 1948 that rattan was again used for ribs in Nantucket baskets. Hickory was always popular since the earliest days, and later on oak also was used for ribs.

Diameter 7 ½ inches   Height 5 ½ inches

DESCRIPTION OF PLATE 26

The last of our group of eight baskets with rattan ribs, this has the two oak ribs with nicely carved ears seen in previous plates. The mahogany lathe-turned bottom has one deep groove on the inside.

The mold shown in this plate is one on which this basket might have been made. It is fashioned of circular pieces cut from two-inch pine planks and then whittled to the proper shape.

What appeared to be fine writing on the handle proved to be merely file marks. But it is sometimes rewarding to look at any flat surfaces with a hand lens.

Diameter 8 ¾ inches   Height 5 ½ inches

DESCRIPTION OF PLATE 27

This work or sewing basket is not only our earliest dated one, 1860, but also is unusual for the use of baleen. This whalebone from the mouth of right whales (and their relatives) was used for corset stays and especially for umbrella ribs.

In this case some inventive basketmaker in Nantucket decided to use the baleen for every other rib, alternating with hickory. The weavers are of rattan, as is the carelessly applied rim lacing. The ribs are nailed to the handmade pine bottom on the outside. Loophandles very neatly made are set into the rim on the outside of the basket.

The bottom is painted gray on the outside and the date 1860 is only visible with a hand lens. Perhaps this was made by a ship captain using some scraps of baleen he had brought home. A very attractive and imaginative basket.

Diameter 10 inches   Height 5 ¼ inches

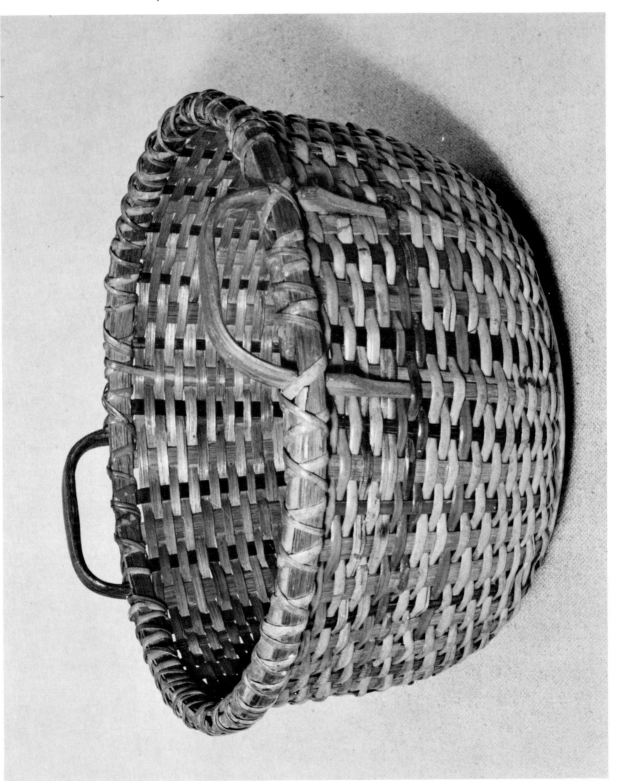

DESCRIPTION OF PLATE 28

A typical Nantucket Lightship basket with oak ribs and handle. The rattan weavers are thin and this basket presents the traditional appearance of the baskets of the latter half of the nineteenth century. It may have been made on board the South Shoal or on land.

The nicely shaped ears are smoothly finished ash wood inserted into the rim and extending halfway down the inside of the basket.

The two pieces of the rim are laced together with rattan very evenly and no attempt is made to hide the nails that are used to attach the ribs to the rim.

The maple bottom is turned with several grooves on the inside. On the outside is printed "L. F. Gardner From Josiah Folger March 15, 1886 Nantuck." A note with the basket says it was perhaps a wedding present. This is one of very few dated baskets.

Diameter 8 ½ inches   Height 5 ¾ inches

DESCRIPTION OF PLATE 29

A large very carefully made basket of hickory ribs and rattan weavers. The sturdy hickory handle is attached to ears of the same material and the area under the rim has been carved in a unique faceted way. Unfortunately this part has been splashed carelessly with red paint, no doubt for identification. The ears have been set into the basket on the outside for only a short distance but the handle remains strong. Flat headed copper rivets and washers, commonly sold for mending leather harness, connect the handle.

Nails appear in the rim as in all baskets from this time on. The mahogany bottom has many deeply cut lathe marks on the inside.

On the outside of the bottom is a note that this was made by Mr. Hosier from Milbrook Farm. Perhaps this basket carried vegetables and fruit.

Diameter 13 inches   Height 8½ inches

DESCRIPTION OF PLATE 30

A very unusual oval basket with hinged mahogany lids. Hinges attached to a center piece of wood allow each side to open. Small handmade hooks and eyes hold the lids firmly.

To allow the lids to fit tightly a flat surface is provided by using flat pieces for the rim. The tapered hickory ribs are nailed at the rim alternately inside and outside.

The strong rigid hickory handle supports the rim with a carved lip. The mahogany bottom being oval would have been made by hand. There are four oval lines drawn on the inside.

There is a note on the bottom saying this was made by "William Hadwen Hosier." The basket in the preceding plate was also by him.

Length 17¼ inches   Width 13 inches   Height 8¼ inches

DESCRIPTION OF PLATE 31

An early nest of seven baskets especially interesting because it is signed and dated. "J. Wyer 1873" is hand carved on the bottoms of all but the smallest basket. Stamped on also is the name "M. E. Starbuck."

Captain James Wyer was master of the ship Spartan and the stepfather mentioned in the book "My House and I" written by Mary Eliza Starbuck who owned this set. In her book she describes her stepfather making lightship baskets in his workshop in the old Walter Folger house on Pleasant Street in Nantucket.

There is a nest similar to this in the Peter Foulger Museum also made by Captain Wyer.

The bottoms are maple, the ribs hickory, the weavers rattan, and the rim pieces and handles are of oak. There is a brass ear proving that these were in use at least as early as 1873.

Diameter 12 inches   Height 7 ¾ inches

DESCRIPTION OF PLATE 32

Two baskets said to be made by Davis Hall who served on the South Shoal Lightship.

The larger one was called a "wood basket." The oval bottom is of maple. The strong rigid handle is chamfered under the rim in a nice design. Davis Hall had a reputation for making very fine baskets.

The smaller basket appears to have been made by the same person although it has a bail handle and a mahogany bottom. The ear carving is the same and also the method of tucking in the lacing.

Length 16¼ inches   Width 12¾ inches   Height 8 inches

Diameter 5½ inches   Height 4½ inches

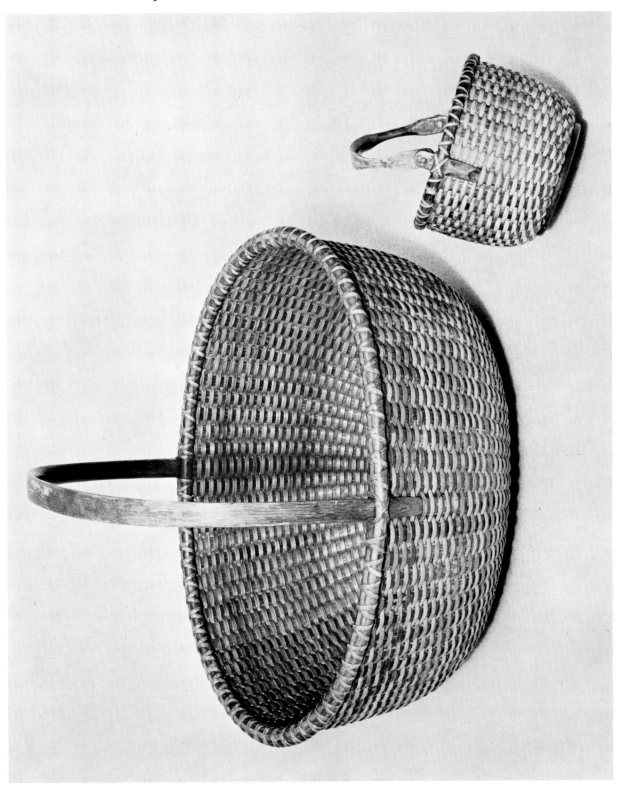

DESCRIPTION OF PLATE 33

Another large basket called a wood basket. Perhaps this was used for kindling split outside and brought into the kitchen.

The mahogany bottom is decorated with very elaborate lathe turnings.

The hickory ribs are very close together which of course strengthens it a great deal.

A very strong and beautiful basket, as useful in the household today as it was a hundred years ago.

Diameter 14¾ inches   Height 9 inches

DESCRIPTION OF PLATE 34

These two very unusual and exceptionally well made baskets have a very artistic treatment of the ear. The rib which extends into the bottom is gradually shaped and rounded until it ends under the rim. The ear itself is smoothed against the handle especially in the smaller basket.

The bottoms are of maple and both turned with the same design which in this case is really a signature, but, alas, of whom we do not know.

Diameter 10 inches   Height 7 inches

Diameter 6¾ inches   Height 4¼ inches

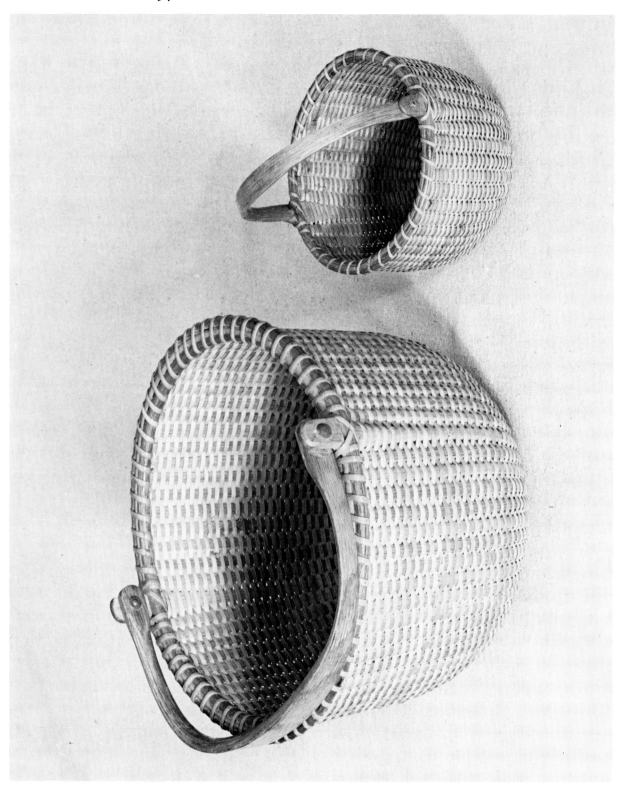

DESCRIPTION OF PLATE 35

A very sturdy "wood" basket which remains as strong today as when it was made. The bottom is turned pine, the handle, rim, and ribs of hickory.

The large ears are carved at the end of a rib, a good method for a large basket.

The good condition of these baskets is a testimony to their high quality of workmanship, and to the care they received. They were obviously appreciated much more than the beaten-up farm baskets seen on the mainland. For the last forty years this has been used for picking beach plums.

Diameter 15¼ inches   Height 10 inches

DESCRIPTION OF PLATE 36

This fine quality sewing basket was made by Captain Thomas James of the South Shoal Lightship. The narrow oak ribs are tapered at the bottom and chamfered slightly at the sides, an example of very painstaking work.

The shallow bowl shape is unusual and being slightly concave near the bottom it gives a very artistic appearance. The lacing of the maple rim is extremely even and the tiny copper nails are put in so they scarcely show. There is one rattan wrapped circular handle.

The cherry bottom has three circles similar to the following two plates which also show baskets by Captain James.

Diameter 10½ inches   Height 4 inches

DESCRIPTION OF PLATE 37

A sewing basket with a stand made by using another basket inverted as the foot. This is also made by Captain Thomas James of the South Shoal Lightship.

There are two small rattan wrapped circular handles. The bottom is of mahogany with a design of three circles which is certainly the mark used by Captain James for identification as it appears in three baskets by him.

The foot basket is very finely woven and has also a mahogany bottom with the same three circles.

Very cleverly devised and executed, this basket must have been on some Nantucket mantelpiece as a decoration rather than for use as a work basket.

Diameter 8 ½ inches   Height 5 inches

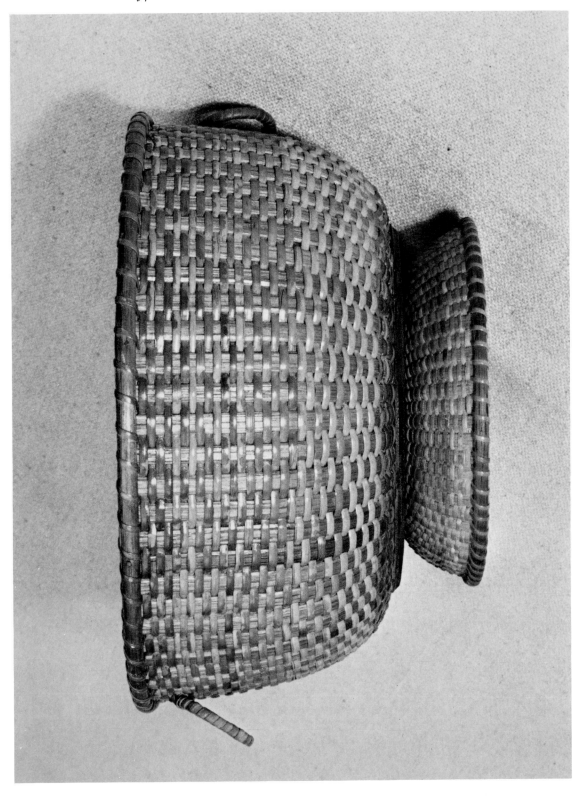

DESCRIPTION OF PLATE 38

A third type of work basket by Captain Thomas James and different especially because of the materials. Small rattan ribs and fine palm leaf strips for weavers give this basket a very unique and fragile appearance.

The palm material was woven into hats by women doing work at home so was available. Captain James shows much inventiveness and originality in his baskets in their shape and in this case in the material. It is not a durable fiber, however, although it does look very elegant.

The bottom is cedar with the same three circles appearing on the two other baskets by Captain James. There are two rattan wrapped, round handles. From its appearance this basket saw little use, and served as an ornament.

Diameter 13 inches   Height 5 inches

DESCRIPTION OF PLATE 39

These two oval baskets are typical of Captain Andrew Sandsbury who served on the South Shoal Lightship for many years. His baskets resemble those by Captain James in their high quality.

The oak ribs are slightly chamfered on the sides and also tapered toward the bottom. The oak bail handles are very beautifully shaped.

The interesting feature in these baskets is the use of sheet brass ears to secure the handles. These were popular on the lightship and become universal towards the latter part of the nineteenth century. The nest of seven baskets made by Captain Wyer and dated 1873 uses these pins in direct contradiction to an early writer who claimed they did not appear before 1900.

Baskets like this are the epitome of the Nantucket tradition. It is possible these two were part of a nest.

Length 12 ½ inches   Width 8 ¼ inches   Height 5 ¼ inches

Length 11 ¼ inches   Width 6 ¾ inches   Height 4 ¾ inches

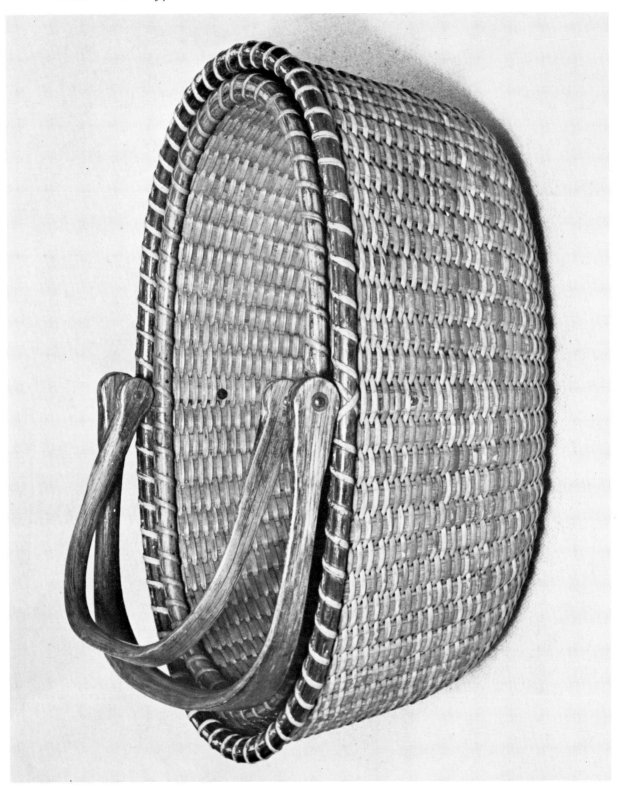

DESCRIPTION OF PLATE 40

Another basket by Captain Sandsbury. This one has a rigid handle with a cutout inside and outside to allow for the rim.

Rattan, dyed black, is used to form a pattern below the rim. There must have been great competition on board as each maker attempted to produce something unusual.

This neat simple basket does have a simplicity which might lead one to say it was influenced by Quakers, but by this time there were very few Friends on the Island. This style depends more on the makers skill and delight in perfecting his craft. Every detail is considered well and executed with care. It is a real object of beauty.

Length 11 inches   Width 7 ¼ inches   Height 4 ½ inches

DESCRIPTION OF PLATE 41

Another oval basket from the South Shoal Lightship this time by Joe Fisher.

The two baskets made by Joe Fisher, this one and one on the following plate have criss-cross lacing and very narrow handles ending in what was called a "snake's head" shape. The bottom is cherry.

He was an associate of Captain Sandsbury and his baskets are of the same fine quality. Joe Fisher left the Lightship in 1892.

Length 10½ inches   Width 7¼ inches   Height 7 inches

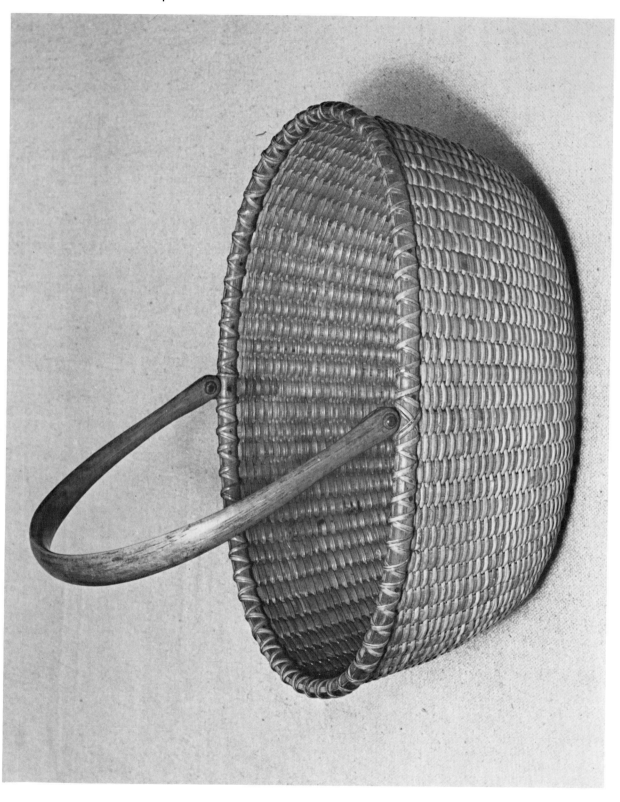

DESCRIPTION OF PLATE 42

An unusual flat round basket by Joe Fisher with maple bottom, hickory ribs, rattan weavers, rattan criss-cross lacing of rim pieces. The handle is very delicately carved similar to the one on the preceding plate.

The ears are brass and the handle must be slit to fasten them in, the method popular on the South Shoal Lightship and on land in the last thirty years of the nineteenth century. Carving the ears as was previously done was time consuming, although it produced much more individual baskets.

Diameter 10 inches   Height 3 ½ inches

DESCRIPTION OF PLATE 43

A very small basket said to be made by William Barnard who lived at the corner of Summer and Pleasant Streets, Nantucket.

There is a mahogany bottom with three circles inside. Perhaps this was one of a nest which became lost; this very often happened and accounts for some odd sizes.

How many baskets were produced on the Island and the lightship? It would be impossible to make any kind of guess but certainly the number would be many thousands, and these have traveled everywhere, sometimes appearing unidentified and unappreciated at stores and auctions.

Diameter 5 inches   Height 3 ½ inches

DESCRIPTION OF PLATE 44

A large bushel basket made with wide oak ribs and wide rattan weavers, ash rim, oak handles, and walnut bottom.

It was made for heavy duty probably on a farm. The three small baskets are hung inside for comparison. They were called one-egg baskets and are two and a half inches high. They were made by Sherwin Boyer and others some fifty years after the bushel.

This basket required a very large mold.

Diameter 17 ½ inches   Height 11 inches

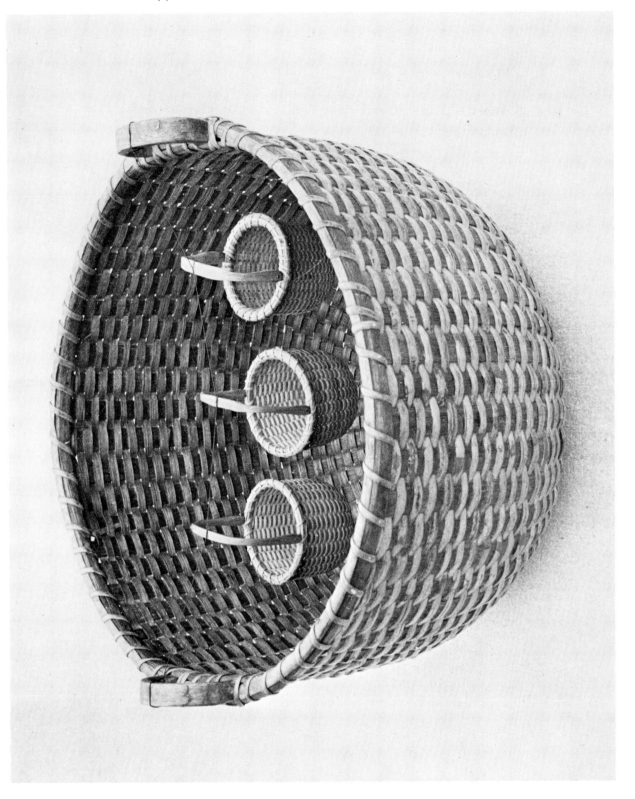

DESCRIPTION OF PLATE 45

A sturdy round nest of seven baskets made by Mitchell Ray. Except for the rattan weavers and lacings and the cherry bottom of the largest, oak is used throughout. The handles have a nice flattened shape which fits well into a nest.

After about 1895 there were no more basket makers on the South Shoal Lightship, but some of the men continued weaving on land. As these men grew old, a new group appeared and by 1920 they were supplying the shops.

One of these was "Mitchy" Ray whose grandfather Captain Charles B. Ray of the South Shoal Lightship had announced he had made 200 baskets by 1866.

"Mitchy" made baskets of all sizes including wastebaskets and oval and round nests.

Diameter 12 ½ inches   Height 10 inches

DESCRIPTION OF PLATE 46

A round basket by Mitchell Ray with his identifying two circles inside the mahogany bottom.

The oak rim is nailed together. The handles and ribs are also oak. The label reads merely "Made by Mitchell Ray Nantucket Mass."

This shape was popular in the twenties and thirties for a workbasket or breadbasket.

Sometimes "Mitchy" Ray's label included the rhyme: "I was made on Nantucket, I'm strong and I'm stout, Don't lose me or burn me and I'll never wear out."

Diameter 10 inches   Height 5 inches

DESCRIPTION OF PLATE 47

The two larger baskets are made by Ferdinand Sylvaro of 97 Orange Street. He worked in the post lightship period in the twenties and thirties, and was a neighbor of Williams and no doubt learned from him. Williams himself is said to have learned from Appleton who also lived on lower Orange Street after he left the South Shoal Lightship. The fine strong wastebasket is of oak with maple bottom and of course rattan weavers. It has no label but the inside of the bottom is incised with three narrow equally spaced circles which were Sylvaro's trademark.

The middle sized basket has both his trademark and his paper label which reads "Made by Ferdinand Sylvaro, Nantucket."

The smallest basket is by Mitchell Ray.

Diameter 11 ¾ inches	Height 11 inches
Diameter 6 ½ inches	Height 3 inches
Diameter 3 ¼ inches	Height 2 ½ inches

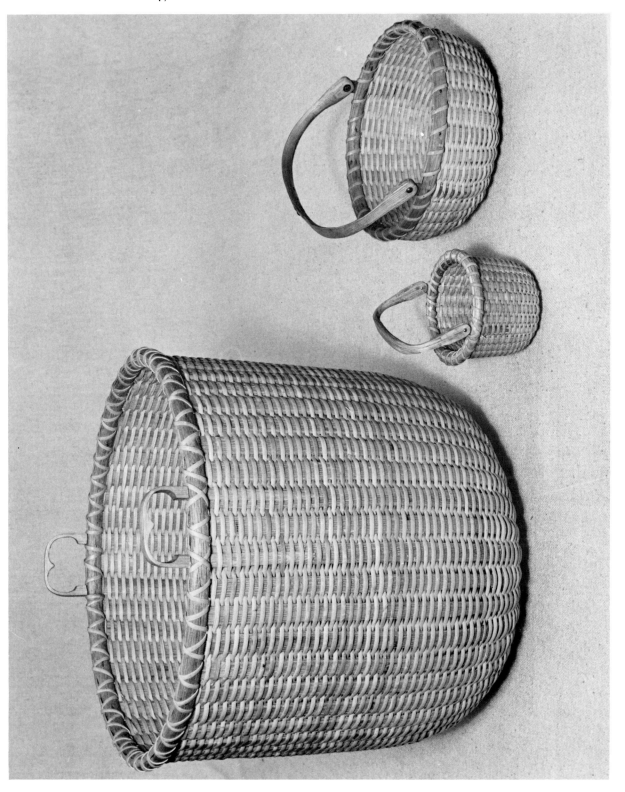

DESCRIPTION OF PLATE 48

An oval nest of seven baskets made by A. D. Williams. Three bottoms are of maple, two of cherry, and two of tulip wood, showing how the men used what came to hand. Handles, ribs, and rims are of oak. The ribs are slightly bevelled to make the weavers fit better; this is true in almost all of the later baskets.

"Light Ship Basket Made by A D Williams Nantucket Mass" appears on the bottom written in black ink. He lived at 120 Orange Street and was famous for the quality of his work.

Length 15 ½ inches   Width 12 ¼ inches   Height 8 ¾ inches

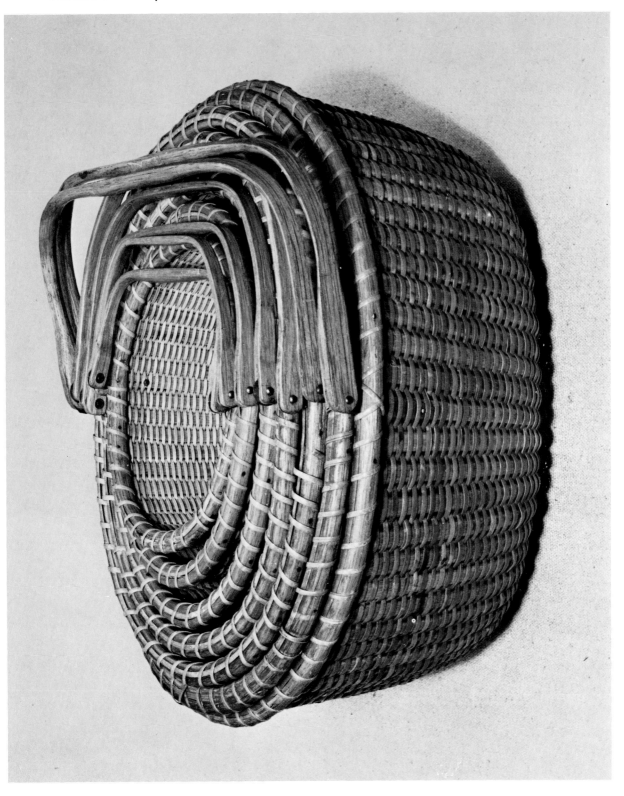

DESCRIPTION OF PLATE 49

Two dated covered baskets. These are fitted with woven lids. The larger one has a maple centerpiece on the lid and a maple bottom. On the blue paper label on the bottom is written "Light Ship Basket Made by A D Williams 120 Orange St Nantucket Mass." The date is stamped on, 1923.

The ears are brass and offset outwards to clear the lid. In both baskets the rims are nailed with brass escutcheon pins. The two baskets are identical in construction except for a mahogany centerpiece in the lid of the small one. The paper label is white and is as above except for the date: Nov. 17 1918. Each lid has a small brass hinge.

These are two elegant baskets foreshadowing the covered handbags of José Reyes.

Diameter 11 inches   Height 8 ½ inches

Diameter 5 ¼ inches   Height 3 ¾ inches

DESCRIPTION OF PLATE 50

Two handbags by José Reyes. Everything except the top, bottom and handle are rattan. The cherry top is ornamented with a black ebony whale by Charles Sayle whose wife was the one who first suggested decorating Mr. Reyes' handbags in this way.

The basket with the ivory whale has ivory pins holding the handle and the latch. The whale is carved by Aletha Macy.

These are examples of Mr. Reyes' early baskets made in the fifties. The label is a map of Nantucket and "Made in Nantucket José Formoso Reyes."

We have come a long way from the early baskets not only in time but in the artistic expression of the craft.

Length 6¾ inches   Width 5 ½ inches   Height 8 inches

Length 8 inches   Width 6 inches   Height 7 inches

DESCRIPTION OF PLATE 51

Three large and beautiful handbags by José Reyes. The three whales carved by Aletha Macy are mounted on ebony. There are two handles with ivory pins, or dowels, and the hasp and pin are also of ivory. This basket is dated 1956.

All three are marked with the map of Nantucket and José Formoso Reyes.

Length 10¾ inches   Width 8¼ inches   Height 7½ inches

The basket with the dolphin carved by Nancy Chase and mounted on walnut has a single handle and is dated 1966.

Length 8 inches   Width 6½ inches   Height 7¼ inches

The basket with the large sea gull carved by Mr. Reyes himself and mounted on gaboon or striped ebony has a complete ivory latch. It is dated 1971.

Length 11 inches   Width 8½ inches   Height 8 inches

There appears to be a great difference between the Indian basket on Plate 1 and these three which are so sophisticated and carefully designed. They are separated by almost two hundred years, but have many basic similarities. Also they are both products of their age; the berry basket represents an early simple life, the Nantucket Lightship Basket handbag is the badge of the modern world which, although so different, still respects and cherishes work that is made by hand.

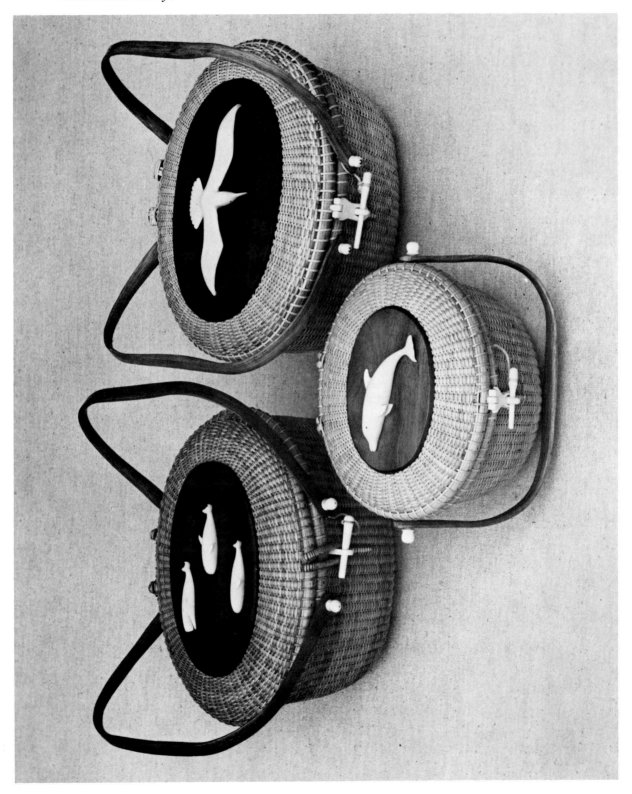

DESCRIPTION OF PLATE 52

A. Materials for basket making. Handle tied to hold its shape. Rattan for weaving (also called cane or reed). Ribs. Three basket bottoms.

B. Three oval basket molds made of soft pine board layers, cut on a jigsaw, glued together, then shaped with a wood rasp. The two on the left have bottoms screwed on, ready for ribs. The right hand one shows the indentation for a bottom.

C. Ribs in place having been soaked, inserted, then held by rubber bands.

D. The beginning of a basket, shown with the bucket which was its mold. These ribs are of "Wide Flat Oval Reed" three-eighths of an inch wide. The shape of the mold is formed by a turned wood pad shown in place on the bucket with a walnut bottom fastened above it. Basket and mold by B. F. D. Runk.

E. Woven basket of Fig. C ready to be removed and fitted with rims. Observe the tapering and fitting of ribs into the bottom.

F. A nearly completed basket showing the use of extended ribs for ears, and rims made of several short pieces fitted together. This needs only the rim cover strip, rim wrappings and a handle to be finished.

G. Sketch to show detail of handle and ears.

H. Finished baskets of several sizes by Paul Willer. The smaller ones have handles pinned to the outside of rims with ivory discs for decoration.

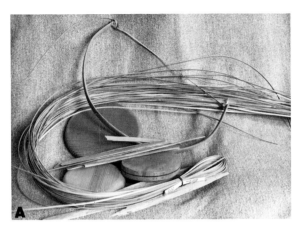

A

B

C

D

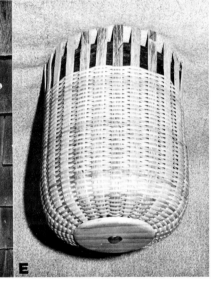

E

F

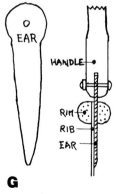

EAR

HANDLE

RIM
RIB
EAR

G

H

Notes for the Second Edition

Since publication of the first edition we have received many letters about baskets. There was, for instance, the California woman who bought a Nantucket lightship basket for three dollars, and the beautiful nest purchased for eighteen dollars near Boston. On the other hand, a nest for four thousand dollars was advertised in a leading magazine. Letters came presenting as Nantucket baskets everything from a boat-shaped Chinese basket to one made by South American Indians.

There were inquiries about preserving these Nantucket baskets and how to rehabilitate an old and dirty one. These really dirty ones should be washed with a brush, dried well, and painted with shellac. Removing paint from a basket is risky unless done carefully by hand. Use a professional caustic bath with caution as one basket we saw had completely collapsed.

Baskets color with age, in different darker shades, but no basket should be colored dark on purpose to simulate aging. A collection of old baskets should be of different tones. Recently we saw a collection where all the baskets were of the same dark color having been treated with a darkening agent. If necessary a light coat of shellac can be painted on an old basket to preserve it.

By far the most letters show an interest in how the baskets are made. While a few people want to make baskets themselves, many are really interested in the details so they can identify them for their collections or shops.

One Nantucketer said, "Don't publish how they are made, it will destroy the mystique." There is no "mystique" to making a lightship basket but there is skill, practice, and a desire to make a handcrafted object of the highest standard. It is this high quality that distinguishes the Nantucket Lightship Baskets of the past and the present. It is this, also, which separates them from the Hong Kong imitations. It is said that imitation is the sincerest kind of flattery but people are often misled into believing they have a genuine article when they do not. Turned out in great quantities with careless workmanship and poor materials these baskets should cost very little and always be properly identified by the seller as Hong Kong imitations.

The following description of making a Nantucket basket is presented with the idea that each person, if he makes one, will use his own ingenuity and inventiveness in interpretation. Some will wish to make an old style basket and for him these directions are expressly made.

Directions for making an eight inch Nantucket Lightship Basket.

The mold: See plates 16, 26, and 52.

In plate 16 the mold is turned on a lathe from a solid piece of wood. In plate 26 the mold is constructed from circular layers of pine glued together and filed or whittled to the proper shape. An indentation may be made to fit the bottom of the basket but this is not necessary.

Various plastic bowls or pails (see plate 52 D) can be used and are inexpensive and simple to work with. In all molds care should be taken to give the proper curve to the basket. A study of old baskets and of the plates in this book will help. The side of the mold should slope inward very gently toward the bottom so the basket will easily come off the mold.

The mold for this basket should be about eight inches in diameter and six and a half inches deep.

The basket bottom: Fine grain physically hard wood makes the sturdiest bottoms but any half inch board (not plywood) will do, such as the ends of pine apple boxes.

Mark a circle on the board with a compass noting carefully the center point where a small hole is drilled so it may be screwed to the mold.

An eight inch basket would need a five inch circular bottom half an inch thick. Cut a slot half an inch deep all around the disk with a hacksaw. The bottom is then sanded and smoothed.

The Ribs: For this basket use thirty-seven ribs half an inch wide, seven and a half inches long and one-sixteenth inch thick. Be sure to make extras in case of breakage. An odd number of ribs is always used to make the weaving come out properly.

Ribs are split or sawed from a straight grain board of oak or ash. Taper each rib about two inches from one end where the curve of the basket will be until at the bottom the width is about five-sixteenths to one-quarter of an inch wide. Bevel or champfer the edges of each rib slightly to allow the weavers to fit better. Sand the ribs smooth. These should be soaked at least overnight before inserting in the bottom. However some may need to be boiled or soaked longer. It is a matter of trial and error.

If using "Wide Flat Oval Reed" the process is easier. Shape each end as above but it will not be necessary to bevel the edges. Soak these ribs about an hour before using.

The Weavers: For this basket "Medium Natural Strand Cane" is needed. The minimum quantity one can buy is half a bunch, or more than enough for three baskets. Select the smoothest and best pieces free of cracks, splits, and blemishes on the shiny or bark side. For convenience each strand is coiled over the fingers to form a small packet. These are kept in a pan of water when the weaving is in process.

The Rims: There are two pieces, one for the inside and one for the outside. They should be at least six inches longer than the circumference of the basket to allow for a tapered lapover or splice of the ends. For this eight inch basket each rim piece should be thirty-three inches at the start. Rims may be made of green stems of oak or hickory split in half and whittled to half-round shape while green. It is important to find a length which has straight grain. Each finished piece should be about three-eighths inches wide and three-sixteenths deep. Whittle the ends on opposite sides to make a neat-fitting lapover of about three inches. Soak them, if green, only overnight and bend into a circle approximately the right size with the flat sides together which allows the half round to be on the outside and inside of the basket. Allow to dry for a day or two.

"Round Reed" simplifies the process enormously. It is easily split, then the ends are shaved for the lapover. Round Reed will soften after being soaked about an hour. Tie in a circle ready to mount on the basket when dry.

The Handle: Use a sapling of oak, hickory, maple or ash. Peel off the bark, cut a piece about sixteen inches and flatten one side for the top. Round the under side. The handle should be approximately five-sixteenth inches thick and half an inch wide. Shape ends of handle, see Plates 39, 41, and 43. Soak two or three days and bend to the right shape to meet the basket edge and tie. Dry for at least a week.

To make the brass ears for the handle cut a piece of thin brass into a slightly tapered strip (Plate 52 G) a little less than the width of one rib and about two and a half inches long. Drill a hole in the rounded top at the proper height to allow the handle to swing easily—in this case about one quarter inch from the top of the ear. Saw a slot in the ends of the handle that will allow the brass piece to extend into the slot about five eighths of an inch. (see Plate 52 G)

Rattan is called Reed or Cane commercially. All types of cane mentioned here may be purchased from H. H. Perkins Co., 10 South Bradley Road, Woodbridge, Conn. 06525 or from other craft supply stores.

Brass strips come in various sizes from Brookstone, Peterborough, N.H. 03458.

Putting the Basket Together

Fasten the basket bottom to the mold with a screw. Insert the ribs into the slot in the bottom and adjust evenly. Using a large heavy rubber band, or a string, contain the ribs against the mold.

Allow the ribs to dry, remove the band and start to weave. To begin weaving thin the end of a cane strip and insert into the slot behind a rib and weave over and under pulling tight but not too tight. Thirty-one rows of weaving should bring the basket to its proper height of five and one half inches. Be sure to work with wet cane. To splice the cane merely thin about three inches of both old and new strips by scraping the inner surface over a knife blade. Place the new strip over the old one for about three inches and continue weaving.

Place the inside rim at the top of the weaving, expand and adjust the lapover to make a neat splice. Mark with pencil where the splice fits, remove, and glue it together. Return it to the basket edge and clamp with clothes pins or Stanley glueing clamps. With small brass escutcheon pins nail the rim to the ribs in four places. Repeat the process for the outside rim using three or four pins to hold it in place.

Mark two opposite places for the handle ears. Slide the ears into the basket so that about five-eighths of an inch extends above the rim. Drill a small hole through rims and ears and drive in a pin. Nail every other rib to the rim. Now cut off the ribs and pin points and smooth with a file. Use a piece of cane as a cover strip between the two rims. It is this refinement of using a strip to cover the rib ends which is one of the distinguishing marks of a lightship basket. Wrap as shown in Plate 52 H and other plates. Tuck in the end of the binding on the inner side of the basket. It was pulled down through the weavers in some old baskets (see Plate 19).

Put the handle over the ear and drill a hole through the wood to match the one in the ear. Heat a copper nail red hot to soften it and with this fasten the handle to the ear using a washer on one side and peen the nail end to fasten the washer.

Sand the basket carefully and paint it with white shellac. A very small amount of orange shellac may be mixed in. The shellac adds firmness to the weaving and strengthens the basket as a whole.

Notes for the Third Edition

There is an increasing interest in crafts in these times and basketmaking of all types has become a very popular hobby. Naturally making a Nantucket Lightship Basket appeals especially to someone who knows the island.

No doubt frequently the motive for making a Lightship Basket is financial. "Why pay so much for a basket when I can make one myself?" they say and proceed to either buy or scrounge supplies asking help sometimes from their professional friends. They buy or beg the bottoms, the ready-prepared ribs, the prepared handle, etc. and settle down to weave. In time, if they are lucky, they have a basket which they proudly say they "made."

Actually what they have done is "assemble" a basket, a perfectly acceptable activity, but quite different from the detailed work of the more professional maker who spends much time in preparation of materials, often including fashioning a mold. When people frequently ask how long it takes to make a basket they are thinking of the weaving which is the least of the work. Hours of preparation go into a basket.

There are many professional makers of Nantucket Lightship Baskets selling their baskets on the island and they deserve praise for the high standard they have maintained.

The following is a list of some of the basketmakers:

WILLIAM AND RUTH BACKSMITH

MIKE BEDELL

G. L. BROWN

PAUL JOHNSON

MICHAEL KANE

CHIN MANASMONTRI

SUSAN AND CARL OTTISON

WILLIAM AND JEANNE REIS

WILLIAM AND JUDY SAYLE

W. SEVRENS

TERRY SYLVIA

PAUL WHITTEN

PAUL WILLER

JUDY YACUS

José Reyes, the dean of the modern basketmakers died on December twenty-fourth 1980.

Basketmaking supplies may be obtained from the following:

H. H. Perkins
10 South Bradley Rd.
Woodbridge, Conn. 06525

Connecticut Cane & Reed Co.
P. O. Box 1276
Manchester
Conn. 06040

New Hampshire Cane & Reed Co.
Daniel Webster Highway
Suncook
New Hampshire 03275

Peerless Rattan
45 Indian Lane
P. O. Box 8
Towaco
New Jersey 07082